and the
GODHEAD

The Divinity of Christ
and the Personhood
of the Holy Spirit

Ellen Gould White

Published by
Return of the Latter Rain Publishers
returnofthelatterrain@gmail.com

Compiled by Raymond Joseph
Cover design by Buffy Joseph and Emily Duffield
Page Design by Emily Duffield

ISBN: 978-1-945933-18-9

TABLE OF CONTENTS

AMAZING FACTS
MINISTRIES

This special edition printed with permission for
Amazing Facts Ministries Inc. Canada

Amazing Facts Ministries Inc.
P.O. Box 449
Creston, BC V0B 1G0
1-888-402-6070
250-402-6070

Visit our website:
www.amazingfactsministries.com

For free Bible study guides visit us online
or call the toll free number.

PREFACE

This collection of statements is not a comprehensive work regarding the Godhead; however, it contains a chronological compilation of much of what Ellen G. White wrote regarding the deity of Christ and the personhood of the Holy Spirit.

This historical review, with appropriate references, demonstrates the development of light and progression of clarity in her understanding of these critical subjects.

The revelation of the divinity of Christ was critical for His ministry to the disciples and is critical to His remnant church.

Shortly before His crucifixion, Jesus found it imperative that His disciples be encouraged by a revelation of His divinity. A careful reading of the context and details of the experience on the Mount of Transfiguration reveals the centrality of the divinity of Christ in the story.

He Was Transfigured
Based on Matt. 17:1-8; Mark 9:2-8; Luke 9:28-36.

"Evening is drawing on as Jesus calls to His side three of His disciples, Peter, James, and John, and leads them across the fields, and far up a rugged path, to a lonely mountainside. The Saviour and His disciples have spent the day in traveling and teaching, and the mountain climb adds to their weariness. Christ has lifted burdens from mind and body of many sufferers; He has sent the thrill of life through their enfeebled frames; but He also is compassed with humanity, and with His disciples He is wearied with the ascent.

"The light of the setting sun still lingers on the mountain top, and gilds with its fading glory the path they are traveling. But soon the light dies out from hill as well as valley, the sun disappears behind the western horizon, and the solitary travelers are wrapped in the darkness of night. The gloom of their surroundings seems in harmony with their sorrowful lives, around which the clouds are gathering and thickening.

"The disciples do not venture to ask Christ whither He is going, or for what purpose. He has often spent entire nights in the mountains in prayer. He whose hand formed mountain and valley is at home with nature, and enjoys its quietude. The disciples follow where Christ leads the way; yet they wonder why their Master should lead them up this toilsome ascent when they are weary, and when He too is in need of rest.

"Presently Christ tells them that they are now to go no farther. Stepping a little aside from them, the Man of Sorrows pours out His supplications with strong crying and tears. He prays for strength to endure the test in behalf of humanity. He must Himself gain a fresh hold on Omnipotence, for only thus can He contemplate the future. *And He pours out His heart longings for His disciples, that in the hour of the power of darkness their faith may not fail.*[1] The dew is heavy upon His bowed form, but He heeds it not. The shadows of night gather thickly about Him, but He regards not their gloom. So the hours pass slowly by. At first the disciples unite their prayers with His in sincere devotion;

---

[1] Note from the publishers: all emphasis of bolded and/or italicized words are added by the publishers unless otherwise noted.

but after a time they are overcome with weariness, and, even while trying to retain their interest in the scene, they fall asleep. Jesus has told them of His sufferings; He has taken them with Him that they might unite with Him in prayer; even now He is praying for them. *The Saviour has seen the gloom of His disciples, and has longed to lighten their grief by an assurance that their faith has not been in vain.* Not all, even of the twelve, can receive the revelation He desires to give. Only the three who are to witness His anguish in Gethsemane have been chosen to be with Him on the mount. *Now the burden of His prayer is that they may be given a manifestation of the glory He had with the Father before the world was, that His kingdom may be revealed to human eyes, and that His disciples may be strengthened to behold it. He pleads that they may witness a manifestation of His divinity that will comfort them in the hour of His supreme agony with the knowledge that He is of a surety the Son of God and that His shameful death is a part of the plan of redemption.*

"*His prayer is heard.* While He is bowed in lowliness upon the stony ground, suddenly the heavens open, the golden gates of the city of God are thrown wide, and holy radiance descends upon the mount, enshrouding the Saviour's form. *Divinity from within flashes through humanity, and meets the glory coming from above.* Arising from His prostrate position, Christ stands in godlike majesty. The soul agony is gone. His countenance now shines 'as the sun,' and His garments are 'white as the light.'"[2]

Christ prayed earnestly for His disciples; His concern was that their faith would not fail in the coming crisis. The manifestation for which He prayed was a clear and powerful revelation of His divinity.

---

[2] Ellen White, *Desire of Ages* (1898), p. 419-421.

An End-Time Revelation

Likewise, here in the "time of the end," as described in Daniel and Revelation, we have a great High Priest in the Divine-human person of Jesus, who even now, intercedes for us in the heavenly sanctuary. Ever since the introduction of the Loud Cry and Latter Rain Message, the Lord has been seeking to strengthen his followers' faith in Him.

In her May 1895 letter to O.A. Olson, Ellen White included the divinity of Christ in her description of the Latter Rain message that God sent through Elders Waggoner and Jones:

"The Lord in His great mercy sent a most precious message to His people through Elders Waggoner and Jones. This message was to bring more prominently before the world the uplifted Saviour, the sacrifice for the sins of the whole world. It presented justification through faith in the Surety; it invited the people to receive the righteousness of Christ, which is made manifest in obedience to all the commandments of God. Many had lost sight of Jesus. *They needed to have their eyes directed to His divine person,* His merits, and His changeless love for the human family. All power is given into His hands, that He may dispense rich gifts unto men, imparting the priceless gift of His own righteousness to the helpless human agent. This is the message that God commanded to be given to the world. It is the third angel's message, which is to be proclaimed with a *loud voice, and attended with the outpouring of His Spirit in a large measure.*"[3]

---

[3] Ellen White, *Testimonies to Ministers*, p. 91-92.

There will soon be great trials coming upon God's people. We believe that clear light on Christ's divinity is coming to our attention, at this time, for this very reason. This is not a coincidence; it is a part of God's plan. Like the disciples, we too need stronger faith, especially now. A progressively clearer understanding of the divine person of Christ is a critical part of strengthening our faith in Him.

In this context, is it helpful to note this statement by Ellen White:

"The truth of God is progressive; it is always onward, going from strength to a greater strength, from light to a greater light. We have every reason to believe that the Lord will send us increased truth, for a great work is yet to be done. … Much has been lost because our ministers and people have concluded that we have had all the truth essential for us as a people; but such a conclusion is erroneous and in harmony with the deceptions of Satan; for truth will be constantly unfolding."[4]

The purpose of this collection of statements is not to promote debate, argument, or theological wrestling, but to promote study on the divinity of Christ for the encouragement and upbuilding of faith in the goodness and power of God, as revealed in and through Christ.

This is the prayer of the publishers for ourselves and for you, dear reader.

The Publishers

---

[4] Ellen White, "Candid Investigation Necessary to an Understanding of the Truth," *Signs of the Times*, May 26, 1890, par. 2.

ELLEN WHITE AND THE GODHEAD

Jesus was equal with God

"This Saviour was the brightness of His Father's glory and the express image of His person. He *possessed divine majesty, perfection, and excellence.* He was *equal with God.* 'It pleased the Father that in Him should all fullness dwell.' 'Who, being in the form of God, thought it not robbery to be equal with God: but made Himself of no reputation…'"[5]

"The extent of the terrible consequences of sin could never have been known, had not the remedy provided been of *infinite value.* The salvation of fallen man was procured at such an immense cost that angels marveled, and could not fully comprehend the divine mystery that the *majesty of Heaven, equal with God*, should die for the rebellious race."[6]

"Angels were filled with amazement and awe, as they knew the world's Redeemer was passing through inexpressible suffering to achieve the redemption of man. He who was *equal with God* in the royal courts, was before them emaciated from nearly six weeks of fasting."[7]

---

[5] Ellen White, *Testimonies for the Church,* vol. 2, (1869), p. 200.
[6] Ellen White, "The First Advent of Christ," *Review & Herald*, December 17, 1872, par. 8.
[7] Ellen White, "The Temptation of Christ," *Review & Herald*, September 1, 1874, par. 14.

"Christ humbled Himself from the highest authority, from the position of *one equal with God*, to the lowest place, that of a servant."[8]

"The salvation of fallen man was procured at such an immense cost that angels marveled, and could not fully comprehend the divine mystery that the Majesty of Heaven, *equal with God*, should die for the rebellious race."[9]

"His divinity was veiled beneath humanity. He hid within himself those *all-powerful attributes which belonged to him* as *one equal with God*. At times his divine character flashed forth with such wonderful power that all who were capable of discerning spiritual things pronounced him the Son of God."[10]

"The reader… may behold Christ, who was *Monarch* in heaven, *equal with God*, coming down to humanity, and working out the plan of redemption, breaking off from man the chains wherewith Satan had bound him, and making it possible for him to regain his godlike manhood."[11]

"Science is too limited to comprehend the atonement; the mysterious and wonderful plan of redemption is so far reaching that philosophy can not explain it; it will ever remain a mystery that the most profound reason can not fathom. If it could be explained by finite wisdom, it would lose its sacredness and

---

[8] Ellen White, *Testimonies for the Church,* vol. 3 (1875), p. 566.

[9] Ellen White, *Spirit of Prophecy*, vol. 2 (1860), p. 11-12.

[10] Ellen White, *Spirit of Prophecy*, vol. 3 (1864), p. 259.

[11] Ellen White, "Bible Study," *Review & Herald,* January 11, 1881, par. 7.

dignity. It is a mystery that *One equal with the eternal Father* should so abase Himself as to suffer the cruel death of the cross to ransom man; and it is a mystery that God so loved the world as to permit His Son to make this great sacrifice."[12]

"Behold the Man of Calvary; behold Him who is *equal with the Father*; behold the Majesty of heaven; behold the King of glory. God's own dearly-beloved Son—He gave Him a freewill offering for us, and here we see the wonderful condescension of the Father."[13]

"He was the majesty of heaven, he was *equal with the Father*, he was the commander of the hosts of angels, yet he died for man the death that was, above all others, clothed with ignominy and reproach."[14]

"The world's Redeemer was *equal with God*. His authority was *as the authority of God*. He declared that he had no existence separate from the Father. The authority by which he spoke, and wrought miracles, was *expressly his own*, yet he assures us that he and the Father are one…"[15]

"Christ did not seek to be thought great, and yet He was the Majesty of heaven, *equal* in dignity and glory *with the infinite God*. He was God manifested in the flesh…. *Infinite* wisdom, *infinite* love, *infinite* justice, *infinite* mercy, depths, heights,

---

[12] Ellen White, "Man's Obligation to God," *Signs of the Times,* April 3, 1884, par. 7.

[13] Ellen White, Manuscript 16, September 19, 1886; in *Sermons and Talks,* vol. 2, p. 31.

[14] Ellen White, "The Work of the Minister," *Review & Herald,* September 11, 1888, par. 10.

[15] Ellen White, "Christ Revealed the Father," *Review & Herald,* January 7, 1890, par. 1.

lengths, breadths, all passing knowledge, are found in Him."[16]

"To save the transgressor of God's law, Christ, the one *equal with the Father*, came to live heaven before men, that they might learn to know what it is to have heaven in the heart."[17]

"The highest angel in heaven had not the power to pay the ransom for one lost soul. Cherubim and seraphim have only the glory with which they are endowed by the Creator as His creatures, and the reconciliation of man to God could be accomplished only through a *mediator* who was *equal with God*, possessed of attributes that would dignify, and declare him worthy to treat with the infinite God in man's behalf, and also represent God to a fallen world."[18]

"The words of our lesson are from the lips of no other than the Majesty of heaven; of him who was *equal with the Father*, one with God."[19]

"It was to save the transgressor from ruin that he who was *co-equal with God*, offered up his life on Calvary."[20]

"Jesus could give alone security to God; for He was *equal with God*. He alone could be a mediator between God and man; for He

---

[16] Ellen White to a Layman in Fresno, CA, Letter 8a, July 7, 1890; in *Manuscript Releases,* vol. 20, p. 94.

[17] Ellen White, "The Teacher of Truth the Only Safe Educator," *Review & Herald,* November 17, 1891, par. 11.

[18] Ellen White, "No Caste in Christ," *Review & Herald,* December 22, 1891, par. 1.

[19] Ellen White, "The Poor in Spirit," *Bible Echo,* May 15, 1892, par. 2.

[20] Ellen White, "Gospel Hearers—No. 5: Good-Ground Hearers," *Review & Herald,* June 28, 1892, par. 3.

possessed divinity and humanity. Jesus could thus give security to both parties for the fulfillment of the prescribed conditions. As the Son of God He gives security to God in our behalf, and as the *eternal Word*, as one *equal with the Father*, He assures us of the Father's love to usward who believe His pledged word."[21]

"One of *infinite dignity*, who was *equal with God*, humbled Himself so that He might meet man in his fallen, helpless condition, and become an advocate before the Father in behalf of humanity."[22]

"He who was *equal with God*, who was *great in counsel*, *mighty in working*, was equal to the emergency that had arrived in the government of God. God sent his Son into the world, not to pass sentence of condemnation upon a rebellious race, but to make manifest his love, and to hold out the hope of eternal life to those who should believe in his Son."[23]

"Jesus was the Commander of heaven, one *equal with God*…. Far higher than any of the angels, *equal with the Father* in dignity and glory, and yet wearing the garb of humanity! Divinity and humanity were mysteriously combined, and man and God became one."[24]

"Christ was not compelled to endure this cruel treatment. The yoke of obligation was not laid upon Him to undertake the work

---

[21] Ellen White, "The Treasure of Truth Rejected," *Review & Herald*, April 3, 1894, par. 13.

[22] Ellen White, "An Example in History," *Review and Herald*, December 17, 1895, par. 8.

[23] Ellen White, "Divinity in Humanity," *Signs of the Times*, March 5, 1896, par. 5.

[24] Ellen White, "Child Life of Jesus," *Signs of the Times*, July 30, 1896, par. 1.

of redemption. Voluntarily He offered Himself, a willing, spotless sacrifice. He was *equal with God, infinite and omnipotent*. He was above all finite requirements. He was Himself the law in character."[25]

"Justice and Mercy stood apart, in opposition to each other, separated by a wide gulf. The Lord our Redeemer clothed his divinity with humanity, and wrought out in behalf of man a character that was without spot or blemish. He planted his cross midway between heaven and earth, and made it the object of attraction which reached both ways, drawing both Justice and Mercy across the gulf. Justice moved from its exalted throne, and with all the armies of heaven approached the cross. There it saw *One equal with God* bearing the penalty for all injustice and sin. With perfect satisfaction Justice bowed in reverence at the cross, saying, It is enough."[26]

"His life was a life of prayer. Yes, Christ, the Son of God, *equal with the Father*, Himself all-sufficient, the storehouse of all blessings, He whose voice could rebuke disease, still the tempest, and call the dead to life, prayed with strong crying and many tears."[27]

"Not one of the angels could have become surety for the human race: their life is God's; they could not surrender it. The angels all wear the yoke of obedience. They are the appointed messengers of Him who is the Commander of all heaven. But Christ is *equal*

---

[25] Ellen White, "Christ as Sacrifice and High Priest," Manuscript 101, 1897; in *Manuscript Releases*, vol. 12, p. 395.

[26] Ellen White, "Christ Our Example - Reading for Sabbath, December 30," *General Conference Daily Bulletin,* October 1, 1899, par. 22.

[27] Ellen White, "Ask, and it Shall be Given You," *Signs of the Times,* September 5, 1900, par. 8.

with God, infinite and omnipotent. He could pay the ransom for man's freedom. He is the eternal self-existing Son, on whom no yoke had come; and when God asked, 'Whom shall I send?' He could reply, 'Here am I; send Me.' He could pledge himself to become man's surety; for He could say that which the highest angel could not say,—I have power over my own life, 'power to lay it down, and… power to take it again.'"[28]

"There are many issues in our world today in regard to the Creator not being a personal God. God is a being, and man was made in His image. After God created man in His image, the form was perfect in all its arrangements, but it had no vitality. Then a personal, *self-existing* God breathed into that form the breath of life, and man became a living, breathing, intelligent being. All parts of the human machinery were put in motion. The heart, the arteries, the veins, the tongue, the hands, the feet, the perceptions of the mind, the senses, were placed under physical law. It was then that man became a living soul."[29]

"In it [the Word] we may learn what our redemption has cost him who was *equal with the Father* from the beginning, and who sacrificed his life that a people might stand before him redeemed from everything earthly and commonplace, renewed in the image of God."[30]

---

[28] Ellen White, "The Price of Our Redemption IV," *Youth's Instructor,* June 21, 1900, par. 2.

[29] Ellen White, "Counsels Regarding Medical Work," Manuscript 117, September 21, 1898; in *Manuscript Releases*, vol. 7, p. 373.

[30] Ellen White, "Counsel to Teachers," *Review & Herald*, November 11, 1909, par. 13.

CHARACTERISTICS OF JESUS

Jesus was self-existent

"Christ was not compelled to endure this cruel treatment. The yoke of obligation was not laid upon Him to undertake the work of redemption. Voluntarily He offered Himself, a willing, spotless sacrifice. He was *equal with God, infinite and omnipotent.* He was above all finite requirements. He was Himself the law in character. Of the highest angels it could not be said that they had never borne a yoke. The angels all bear the yoke of dependence, the yoke of obedience. They are the appointed messengers of Him who is Commander of all heaven.

"No one of the angels could become a substitute and surety for the human race, for their life is God's; they could not surrender it. On Christ alone the human family depended for their existence. He is the *eternal, self-existent Son*, on whom no yoke had come. When God asked, 'whom shall I send, and who will go for Us?' Christ alone of the angelic host could reply, 'Here am I; send Me.' He alone had covenanted before the foundation of the world to become a surety for man. He could say that which not the highest angel could say—'I have power over My own life. I have power to lay it down, and I have power to take it again' [see John 10:18]."[31]

---

[31] Ellen White, "Christ as a Sacrifice and High Priest," Manuscript 101, 1897; in *Manuscript Releases*, vol. 12, p. 395.

"Silence fell upon the vast assembly. The name of God, given to Moses to express the idea of the eternal presence, had been claimed as His own by this Galilean Rabbi. He had announced Himself to be the *self-existent* One, He who had been promised to Israel, 'whose goings forth have been from of old, from the days of eternity.' Mic. 5: 2, margin."[32]

" 'I *am* he that liveth, and was dead; and, behold, I am alive for evermore, Amen; and have the keys of hell and of death. Write the things which thou hast seen, and the things which are, and the things which shall be hereafter; The mystery of the seven stars which thou sawest in my right hand, and the seven golden candlesticks. The seven stars are the angels of the seven churches: and the seven candlesticks which thou sawest are the seven churches' Rev. 1:18-20. These are wonderfully solemn and significant statements. It was the Source of all mercy and pardon, peace and grace, *the selfexistent, eternal, unchangeable One,* who visited His exiled servant on the isle that is called Patmos."[33]

" 'Before Abraham was, I am.' Christ is the pre-existent, *self-existent* Son of God. The message He gave to Moses to give to the children of Israel was, "Thus shalt thou say unto the children of Israel, I Am hath sent me unto you." The prophet Micah writes of Him, 'But thou, Bethlehem Ephratah, though thou be little among the thousands of Judah, yet out of Thee shall He come forth unto Me that is to be ruler in Israel; whose goings forth have been from of old, from everlasting.' "[34]

---

[32] Ellen White, *Desire of Ages* (1898), p. 469-470.

[33] Ellen White, Manuscript 81, 1900, in *SDA Bible Commentary*, vol. 7 (Washington, D.C.: Review & Herald, 1957), p. 955.

[34] Ellen White, "Resistance to Light. No. 3 (Concluded)," *Signs of the Times*, August 29, 1900, par. 13.

"Upon the throne *with the eternal, self-existent One*, is he who 'hath borne our griefs, and carried our sorrows,' who 'was in all points tempted like as we are, yet without sin,' that he might be 'able to succor them that are tempted.'"[35]

"The King of the universe summoned the heavenly hosts before Him, that in their presence He might set forth the true position of His Son and show the relation He sustained to all created beings. The Son of God shared the Father's throne, and the glory of *the eternal, self-existent One encircled both*. About the throne gathered the holy angels, a vast, unnumbered throng—'ten thousand times ten thousand, and thousands of thous-ands' (Revelation 5: 11.), the most exalted angels, as ministers and subjects, rejoicing in the light that fell upon them from the presence of the Deity."[36]

"Jehovah, the *eternal, self-existent, uncreated One*, Himself the Source and Sustainer of all, is alone entitled to supreme reverence and worship. Man is forbidden to give to any other object the first place in his affections or his service."[37]

"God desires His people to look to Him for guidance that they may be led by His Spirit. He is the *eternal, self-existent* Source of all life, physical and Spiritual."[38]

---

[35] Ellen White, *Great Controversy* (1911), p. 416.

[36] Ellen White, *Patriarchs & Prophets* (1890), p. 36.

[37] *Ibid.,* p. 305.

[38] Ellen White to Elder E.E. Franke, Letter 19, January 1901; in *Manuscript Releases,* vol. 21, p. 272.

Christ was God

"In carrying out his enmity to Christ, until He hung upon the cross of Calvary, with wounded, bruised body and broken heart, Satan completely uprooted himself from the affections of the universe. It was then seen that God had in His Son denied himself, giving himself for the sins of the world, because He loved mankind. The Creator was revealed in the Son of the infinite God. Here the question, "Can there be self-denial with God?" was forever answered. *Christ was God*, and condescending to be made flesh, He assumed humanity and became obedient unto death, that He might undergo infinite sacrifice."[39]

Christ was God in the Highest Sense

"The world was made by him, 'and without him was not anything made that was made.' If Christ made all things, he existed before all things. The words spoken in regard to this are so decisive that no one need be left in doubt. *Christ was God essentially, and in the highest sense.* He was with God from all eternity, God over all, blessed forevermore."[40]

From Everlasting

"When reviled, He threatened not; when falsely accused, He opened not His mouth. He prays on the cross for His murderers. He is dying for them. He is paying an infinite price for every one

---

[39] Ellen White, "Christ our High Priest," *Manuscript 50,* March 28, 1900; in *Selected Messages*, book 1, p. 342.

[40] Ellen White, "The Word Made Flesh," *Review & Herald,* April 5, 1906, par. 6.

of them. He would not lose one whom He has purchased at so great cost. He gives Himself to be smitten and scourged without a murmur. And this uncomplaining victim is the Son of God. His *throne* is *from everlasting*, and His kingdom shall have no end.[41]

"When reviled, He threatens not; when falsely accused, He opens not His mouth. He prays on the cross for His murderers. He is dying for them; He is paying an infinite price for every one of them. He bears the penalty of man's sins without a murmur. And this uncomplaining victim is the Son of God. His *throne* is *from everlasting*, and His kingdom shall have no end."[42]

"As the nations of the saved look upon their Redeemer, and behold the eternal glory of the Father shining in his countenance; as they behold his *throne*, which is *from everlasting* to everlasting, and know that his kingdom is to have no end, they break forth in rapturous song…"[43]

"What is the work of angels in comparison with His condescension? His *throne* is *from everlasting*. He has reared every arch and pillar in nature's great temple. Behold Him, the beginning of the creation of God, who numbers the stars, who created the worlds— among which this earth is but a small speck, and would scarcely be missed from the many worlds more than a tiny leaf from the forest trees."[44]

---

[41] Ellen White, "Rest for the Weary," *Review & Herald,* August 2, 1881, par. 10.

[42] Ellen White, "Rest in Christ," *Signs of the Times*, March 17, 1887, par. 11.

[43] Ellen White, *Spirit of Prophecy*, vol. 4, (1884), p. 468.

[44] Ellen White, Manuscript 75, 1886; in *Heavenly Places,* p. 40.

"Think of the Saviour upon the cross, bruised, smitten, mocked, yet uncomplaining and unresisting, suffering without a murmur. This is the Lord of heaven, whose *throne* is *from everlasting*. All this suffering and shame He endured for the joy that was set before Him—the joy of bringing to men the gift of eternal life."[45]

"Jesus had been *with* the Father *from the everlasting ages*, before the creation of man, and He came to reveal the Father, declaring, 'God is love.'"[46]

Not only has He been with the Father, but His love for us has been from everlasting: "Christ's love is matchless, and is exhibited in doing and enduring. It is not possible to trace this love back to the beginning. For ages his eye has been upon us. To all intents and purposes, he was slain for us. He had a kingdom prepared for us before the foundation of the world. His love has been of old, even *from everlasting*. Through the human heart of Christ, the very holiness of God was offered to the young ruler."[47]

From everlasting, Jesus was our Mediator. "But while God's Word speaks of the humanity of Christ when upon this earth, it also speaks decidedly regarding his pre-existence. The Word existed as a divine being, even as the eternal Son of God, in union and oneness with his Father. *From everlasting* he was the *Mediator* of the covenant, the one in whom all nations of the

---

[45] Ellen White, "An Exceeding and Eternal Weight of Glory," *Review & Herald*, May 6, 1902, par. 10.

[46] Ellen White, "Christ's Mission to the World," *Signs of the Times*, June 27, 1892, par. 1.

[47] Ellen White, "One Thing Thou Lackest, No. I" *Youth's Instructor*, May 20, 1897, par. 12.

earth, both Jews and Gentiles, if they accepted him, were to be blessed."[48]

"God and Christ knew from the beginning of the apostasy of Satan and of the fall of Adam through the deceptive power of the apostate. The plan of salvation was designed to redeem the fallen race, to give them another trial. Christ was appointed to the office of *Mediator* from the creation of God, set up *from everlasting* to be our substitute and surety."[49]

" 'Before the mountains were brought forth, or ever thou hadst formed the earth and the world, even f*rom everlasting to everlasting*, thou art God' (Ps. 90: 2). 'The people which sat in darkness saw great light; and to them which sat in the region and shadow of death light is sprung up' (Matt. 4: 16). Here the pre-existence of Christ and the purpose of His manifestation to our world are presented as living beams of light from the eternal throne."[50]

"Christ is *from everlasting to everlasting*, a present help to all who seek Him diligently. And those who seek Him diligently will find Him."[51]

Life Original, Unborrowed, Underived

"Our life is something we receive from Christ by a study of his Word. 'In him was life,' *original, unborrowed*. He was the

---

[48] Ellen White, "The Word Made Flesh," *Review & Herald,* April 5, 1906, par. 5.
[49] *Ibid.,* par. 13.
[50] Ellen White, "The Word Made Flesh," *Review & Herald,* April 5, 1906, par. 9.
[51] Ellen White, Manuscript 20, 1913; in *Sermons and Talks,* vol. 2, p. 339.

Fountain of life. We receive life from the Saviour which he takes back again. That life which God has given us should be put to the very best account; for as human agents we are forming our own destiny."[52]

" 'In him was life; and the life was the light of men' (John 1:4). It is not physical life that is here specified, but immortality, the life which is exclusively the property of God. The Word, who was with God, and who was God, had this life. Physical life is something which each individual receives. It is not eternal or immortal; for God, the Life-giver, takes it again. Man has no control over his life. But the life of Christ was *unborrowed*. No one can take this life from Him. 'I lay it down of myself' (John 10:18), He said. In Him was life, *original, unborrowed, underived*. This life is not inherent in man. He can possess it only through Christ. He cannot earn it; it is given him as a free gift if he will believe in Christ as His personal Saviour."[53]

"Still seeking to give a true direction to her faith, Jesus declared, 'I am the resurrection, and the life.' In Christ is life, *original, unborrowed, underived*. 'He that hath the Son hath life.' 1 John 5:12. The divinity of Christ is the believer's assurance of eternal life."[54]

"In Jesus is our life *derived*. In him is life, that is *original, unborrowed, underived* life. In us there is a streamlet from the

[52] Ellen White, Manuscript 2, February 9, 1896, p. 2-3.
[53] Ellen White, "Christ the Life-giver," *Signs of the Times*, April 8, 1897; in *Selected Messages,* book 1, p. 296.
[54] Ellen White, *Desire of Ages* (1898), p. 530.

fountain of life. In him is the fountain of life. Our life is something that we receive, something that the Giver takes back again to himself. If our life is hid with Christ in God, we shall, when Christ shall appear, also appear with him in glory."[55]

"The ability and wisdom of any man is only derived from God. Connected with God, his life bound up with God, he will work the works of God. God has wisdom *underived*. He is the Infinite One; the human is finite, erring. He is the Fountain of the light and life and glory of the world."[56]

"As our Creator and Redeemer, Christ has embraced the world in His arms of infinite love. All things belong to Him by *original* and mediatorial efficiency. He is the first and the last, and the efficiency of everything. All the value that there is in any human being is from Christ, and all belongs to Him. All that we have was entrusted to us in order to fulfill His mediatorial plan."[57]

---

[55] Ellen White to Brother and Sister Burden, Letter 309, November 1, 1905; in *Medical Ministry*, p. 7.

[56] Ellen White, Manuscript 40, 1890; in *Ellen G. White 1888 Material*, p. 919.

[57] Ellen White, "The Co-operation of Humanity with Divinity," *Signs of the Times,* April 22, 1903, par. 1.

"I AM"
GOD AND CHRIST

"It was no human influence or power Moses possessed, which wrought on the minds, that produced those miracles before Pharaoh. It was the power of God. These signs and wonders were wrought through Moses, to convince Pharaoh that *the great 'I am'* sent him to command Pharaoh to let Israel go, that they might serve him."[58]

" 'Your father Abraham rejoiced to see my day; and he saw it, and was glad.' The Jews listened incredulously to this assertion, and said, sneeringly, 'Thou art not yet fifty years old, and hast thou seen Abraham?' Jesus, with a lofty dignity that sent a thrill of conviction through their guilty souls, answered, 'Verily, verily, I say unto you, *Before Abraham was, I am.*' For a moment, silence fell upon all the people, as the grand and awful import of these words dawned upon their minds. But the Pharisees, speedily recovering from the influence of his words, and fearing their effect upon the people, commenced to create an uproar, railing at him as a blasphemer. 'Then took they up stones to cast at him; but Jesus hid himself, and went out of the temple, going through the midst of them, and so passed by.' "[59]

---

[58] Ellen White, "Phrenology, Psychology, Mesmerism, and Spiritualism," *Review & Herald*, February 18, 1862, par. 5.

[59] Ellen White, *Spirit of Prophecy*, vol. 2 (1860), p. 357-358.

"Although Jesus gave evidence of his divine power, yet he was not permitted to teach his lessons without interruption. The rulers sought to hold him up to ridicule before the people. They would not allow him to state his ideas and doctrines in a connected way, but, although frequently interrupted, light flashed into the mind of hundreds, and when the rulers heard the words of Jesus, that were clothed with power and held the people spellbound, they were angry, and said, 'Thou art a Samaritan, and hast a devil.' Jesus met these charges with quiet dignity, fearlessly and decidedly claiming that covenant rights were centered in himself, and were not received through Abraham. He declared, '*Before Abraham was, I am.*' The fury of the Jews knew no bounds, and they prepared to stone him, but the angels of God, unseen by men, hurried him out of their assembly."[60]

"But many feel that they cannot go to Jesus in confidence. They say: "It does not seem as if God heard my prayers. I have tried and tried to rid my soul of sin, but I cannot do it." Then say, "Lord, I am powerless, and I cast my helpless soul on thee." That is what Jacob did. All night long he had been wrestling with One whom he supposed was his enemy, but it was *the great I AM*, the mighty God, the Prince of peace, and just as long as he continued his wrestling, he found no comfort, no hope. It was a life-and-death question with him, and his strength was almost exhausted. Then the Angel touched his thigh, and he knew that he wrestled with no common adversary. Wounded and helpless, he fell upon the One with whom he had wrestled, just as you and I must do, just as any soul does when he falls upon the Rock and is broken. 'Let me go, for the day breaketh,' pleaded the Angel, but Jacob ceases

---

[60] Ellen White, "Candid Investigation Necessary to an Understanding of the Truth," *Signs of the Times,* May 26, 1890, par. 11.

not his intercession, and Christ has to make terms with this helpless soul. He cannot tear himself away from a soul wounded and helpless, and crying unto him for help. And Jacob pleads, with determined spirit, 'I will not let thee go, except thou bless me.' Who was it that inspired his spirit of persistence?—It was He who wrestled with him, it was He who gave him the victory, who changed his name from Jacob to Israel, and said, 'As a prince hast thou power with God and with men, and hast prevailed.'"[61]

"*God always has been.* He is *the great I AM.* The psalmist declares, 'Before the mountains were brought forth, or ever thou hadst formed the earth and the world, even from everlasting to everlasting, thou art God.' Ps. 90: 2. He is the high and lofty One that inhabiteth eternity. 'I am the Lord, I change not,' He declares. With Him there is no variableness, neither shadow of turning. He is '*the same yesterday, and today and for ever.*' Heb. 13:8. He is *infinite and omnipresent.* No words of ours can describe His greatness and majesty."[62]

" 'God is love' is written upon every soul who will receive the superscription. Jesus, the Majesty of heaven, will unite all souls to Himself who will permit Him to bind them to His great heart of infinite love. Jesus teaches us that God is an *everpresent 'I Am.'* It is by cordially believing that we maintain our allegiance to God. Jesus said, 'As Moses lifted up the serpent in the wilderness, even so must the Son of man be lifted up, that whosoever believeth in Him should not perish, but have everlasting life.' Again He said,

---

[61] Ellen White, " 'Ye are Complete in Him' ", *Signs of the Times*, February 22, 1892, par. 3.

[62] Ellen White, Manuscript 132, 1902; in *Medical Missionary*, p. 92.

'I am the good shepherd…. I lay down My life for the sheep.' 'I am the living bread which came down from heaven: if any man eat of this bread, he shall live for ever: and the bread that I will give is My flesh, which I will give for the life of the world.'"[63]

"*I AM* means an *eternal presence*; the past, present, and future are alike with God. He sees the most remote events of past history, and the far distant future with as clear a vision as we do those things which are transpiring daily. We know not what is before us, and if we did, it would not contribute to our eternal welfare. God gives us an opportunity to exercise faith and trust in *the great I AM*.

"The Lord must keep the city, except the watchman labor in vain. This wonderful truth was revealed by Christ during His mission on earth. Our Saviour says, 'Your father Abraham rejoiced to see my day: and he saw it, and was glad.' Fifteen hundred years before Christ laid off His royal robe, His kingly crown, and left His position of honor in the heavenly courts, assumed humanity and walked a man among the children of men, Abraham saw His day, and was glad.

" 'Then said the Jews unto him, Thou art not yet fifty years old, and hast thou seen Abraham? Jesus said unto them, Verily, verily, I say unto you, Before Abraham was, *I am*. Then took they up stones to cast at him' because of that saying. *Christ was using the great name of God* that was given to Moses to express the idea of the *eternal presence*.

"Isaiah also saw Christ, and his prophetic words are full of significance. He says, 'For unto us a child is born, unto us a Son is given: and the government shall be upon his shoulders: and his

---

[63] Ellen White to Edson and Emma White, Letter 92, February 17, 1895; in *Manuscript Releases*, vol. 19, p. 211.

name shall be called Wonderful, Counselor, The mighty God, The Everlasting Father, The Prince of Peace.'

"Speaking through him, the Lord says, 'I am the Lord thy God, the Holy One of Israel, thy Saviour: I gave Egypt for thy ransom, Ethiopia and Seba for thee. Since thou wast precious in my sight, thou hast been honorable, and I have loved thee: Therefore I will give men for thee, and people for thy life. Fear not: for I am with thee: I will bring thy seed from the east, and gather thee from the west; I will say to the north, Give up; and to the south, Keep not back: bring my sons from far, and my daughters from the ends of the earth; every one that is called by my name; for I have created him for my glory, I have formed him; yea I have made him....'"

"The Pharisees were horrified at this declaration of Christ's, 'Before Abraham was *I am*.' They were beside themselves with rage that He should express such awful blasphemy, *claiming to be the I AM*. They would have stoned Him then and there, but *the I AM* blinded their eyes that they should not see Him, although He went out of the temple, passing through the very midst of them. As Jesus passed through the multitude He saw a man who had been blind from his birth and healed him.

"When Jesus came to our world, He proclaimed Himself, '*I am the way, the truth, and the life: no man cometh unto the Father, but by me.*' 'Hereafter ye shall see heaven opened and the angels of God ascending and descending upon the Son of man.'...

"The Lord must be believed and served as *the great 'I AM,'* and we must trust implicitly in Him."[64]

"In *Christ Jesus* is a revelation of the *glory of the Godhead*. All that the human agent can know of God to the saving of the soul,

---

[64] Ellen White to J. E. and Emma White, Letter 119, February 18 and 19, 1895; in *Manuscript Releases*, vol. 14, p. 21-25.

is the measure of the knowledge of the truth as it is in Jesus, to which he can attain; for Christ is he who represents the Father. The most wonderful truth to be grasped by men is the truth, 'Immanuel, God with us.' Christ is the wisdom of God. *He* is the *great 'I Am'* to the world. As we contemplate the glory of the divine character as revealed in Christ, we are led to exclaim, 'O the depth of the riches both of the wisdom and knowledge of God!' This wisdom is displayed in the love that reaches out for the recovery of lost and ruined man."[65]

"The truth of the third angel's message has been proclaimed by some as a dry theory. But we must all place in that message Christ, as the first and the last, *the I am*, the bright and morning Star."[66]

"By His humanity, Christ touched humanity; by His divinity, He lays hold upon the throne of God. As the Son of man, He gave us an example of obedience; as the Son of God, He gives us power to obey. *It was Christ* who from the bush on Mount Horeb spoke to Moses saying, '*I AM THAT I AM*…. Thus shalt thou say unto the children of Israel, *I Am* hath sent me unto you.' Ex. 3:14. This was the pledge of Israel's deliverance. So when He came 'in the likeness of men,' He *declared Himself the I AM*. The Child of Bethlehem, the meek and lowly Saviour, is God 'manifest in the flesh.' 1 Tim. 3:16. And to us He says: '*I AM* the Good Shepherd.' '*I AM* the living Bread.' '*I AM* the Way, the Truth, and the Life.' 'All power is given unto Me in heaven and in earth.' John 10:11; 6:51; 14:6; Matt. 28:18. *I AM* the assurance of every promise. *I AM*;

---

[65] Ellen White, "Character of the Law Revealed in Christ's Life," *Signs of the Times,* December 12, 1895, par. 5.

[66] Ellen White, "The Love of God," *Signs of the Times,* December 23, 1897, par. 13.

be not afraid. 'God with us' is the surety of our deliverance from sin, the assurance of our power to obey the law of heaven....

"God has adopted human nature in the person of His Son, and has carried the same into the highest heaven. It is the 'Son of man' who shares the throne of the universe. It is the 'Son of man' whose name shall be called, 'Wonderful, Counselor, The mighty God, The everlasting Father, The Prince of Peace.' Isa. 9:6. The *I AM* is the Daysman between God and humanity, laying His hand upon both. He who is 'holy, harmless, undefiled, separate from sinners,' is not ashamed to call us brethren. Heb. 7:26; 2:11. In Christ the family of earth and the family of heaven are bound together. Christ glorified is our brother. Heaven is enshrined in humanity, and humanity is enfolded in the bosom of Infinite Love."[67]

"The Shekinah had departed from the sanctuary, but in the Child of Bethlehem was veiled the glory before which angels bow. This unconscious babe was the promised seed, to whom the first altar at the gate of Eden pointed. This was Shiloh, the peace giver. It was He who declared Himself to Moses as *the I am*. It was He who in the pillar of cloud and of fire had been the guide of Israel. This was He whom seers had long foretold. He was the Desire of all nations, the Root and the Offspring of David, and the Bright and Morning Star."[68]

"With solemn dignity Jesus answered, 'Verily, verily, I say unto you, Before Abraham was, *I Am.*'

"Silence fell upon the vast assembly. The name of God, given to Moses to express the idea of the *eternal presence*, had been *claimed as His own* by this Galilean Rabbi. He had announced

---

[67] Ellen White, *Desire of Ages* (1898), p. 24-26.
[68] *Ibid.*, p. 52.

Himself to be *the self-existent One*, He who had been promised to Israel, 'whose goings forth have been from of old, from the days of eternity.' Mic. 5:2, margin."[69]

---

[69] Ellen White, *Desire of Ages* (1898), p. 469-470.

CHRIST IS JEHOVAH

"The scribes and Pharisees accused Christ of blasphemy because He made Himself *equal with God*. But He promptly met and denied their accusations…. 'Your Father Abraham rejoiced to see My day, and he saw it, and was glad. Then said the Jews unto Him, Thou art not yet fifty years old, and hast Thou seen Abraham? Jesus said unto them, Verily, verily, I say unto you, Before Abraham was, *I am*.'

"Here Christ shows them that, although they might reckon His life to be less than fifty years, yet His divine life could not be reckoned by human computation. The *existence of Christ before His incarnation is not measured by figures.*

"'Before Abraham was, *I am*.' Abraham greatly desired to see the Messiah in His day. He offered up the most earnest prayer that he might see Him before He died. 'He looked for a city which hath foundations, whose builder and maker is God.'….

"But *Abraham saw Christ*. A supernatural light was given him, and he acknowledged Christ's divine character. He had a distinct view of Christ, the Messiah. He saw His day, and was glad. He was given a view of the divine Sacrifice for sin. *It was Jesus Christ* that had promised him, 'Look now toward heaven, and tell the stars, if thou be able to number them; and He said unto him, So shall thy seed be.'…

"'Jesus said unto them, Verily, verily, I say unto you, Before Abraham was, *I am*. Then took they up stones to cast at Him; but Jesus hid Himself, and went out of the temple, going through the midst of them, and so passed by.' What a history is this! The Jews were so blinded by the deception of the enemy that, without any form of trial, they would have stoned Christ to death. They saw that *He made Himself equal with God*, and because they had no knowledge of God or of Jesus Christ, they thought this to be blasphemy. Had they had a knowledge of God, they would not have rejected His Son, and charged Him with blasphemy….

"The *incarnate I AM* is our abiding Sacrifice. The *I AM* is our Redeemer, our Substitute, our Surety. He is the Daysman between God and the human soul, our Advocate in the courts of heaven, our unwearying Intercessor, pleading in our behalf His merits and His atoning sacrifice. *The I AM* is our Saviour. In Him our hopes of eternal life are centered. He is an everpresent help in time of trouble. In Him is the assurance of every promise. We must acknowledge and receive this *almighty Saviour*; we must behold Him, that we may be like Him in character. 'As many as received Him, to them gave He power to become the sons of God, even to them that believe on His name.'"…

"*Jehovah is the name given to Christ.* 'Behold, God is my salvation,' writes the prophet Isaiah; 'I will trust, and not be afraid; for the Lord *JEHOVAH* is my strength and my song; He also is become my salvation. Therefore with joy shall ye draw water out of the wells of salvation. And in that day ye shall say, Praise the Lord, call upon His name, declare His doings among the people, make mention that His name is exalted." "In that day shall this song be sung in the land of Judah: We have a strong city; salvation will God appoint for walls and bulwarks. Open ye the gates, that the righteous nation which keepeth the truth may enter in. Thou wilt keep him in perfect peace whose mind is stayed on Thee, because he trusteth in Thee. Trust ye in the Lord forever; for in the Lord *JEHOVAH* is everlasting strength.'"[70]

---

[70] Ellen White, "The Word Made Flesh," *Signs of the Times,* May 3, 1899, par. 3-18.

"To Moses Jehovah declared, I AM that I am. Christ declared, *'Before Abraham was, I am.'* By this declaration he laid open the resources of his infinite nature, imparting in his words assurance of pardon for the guilty race. He is the Word, conscious of power that He can take up and lay down his life as he chooses, to secure the salvation of those who have fallen under Satan's falsehoods and intrigues."[71]

" 'Then said the Jews unto Him, Thou art not yet fifty years old, and hast Thou seen Abraham?' 'Verily, verily, I say unto you,' Jesus answered, *'Before Abraham was, I am.* Then took they up stones to cast at Him; but Jesus hid Himself, and went out of the temple, going through the midst of them, and so passed by.' Their eyes were blinded that they might not see Him.

" 'Before Abraham was, *I am.'* Christ is the pre-existent, self-existent Son of God. The message He gave to Moses to give to the children of Israel was, 'Thus shalt thou say unto the children of Israel, *I AM* hath sent me unto you.' The prophet Micah writes of Him, 'But thou, Bethlehem Ephratah, though thou be little among the thousands of Judah, yet out of Thee shall He come forth unto Me that is to be ruler in Israel; whose goings forth have been from of old, from everlasting.' "[72]

---

[71] Ellen White to William Kerr, Letter 79, May 10, 1900; in *The Upward Look*, p. 144.

[72] Ellen White, "Resistance to Light. No. 3 (Concluded)," *Signs of the Times*, August 29, 1900, par. 12-13.

Chronological Summary

Below is a list of statements made by Ellen White concerning the Deity of Christ, in chronological order.

- 1SG 77, 1858 — The Lord of Hosts
- RH, Feb. 18, 1862 — "The great I AM" applied to God
- 2T, 200, 1869 — Christ possessed divine majesty, perfection and excellence
- 2T, 200, 1869 — Christ equal with God
- RH, Dec. 17, 1872 — The majesty of Heaven
- 2SP 358, 1877 — Grand and awful import of "before Abraham was I am"
- 3SP, 259, 1878 — All-powerful attributes
- RH Aug. 8, 1878 — "The eternal Son of God"
- RH, Jan. 11, 1881 — Monarch in heaven
- RH, Aug. 2, 1881 — His throne is from everlasting
- 4SP, 24 1884— God himself manifest in the flesh
- BE, Mar. 8, 1887 — "the eternal Word"
- MS 17, 1890 — God over all
- ST, Aug. 24, 1891 — Redemption arranged with Christ from all eternity
- ST, Feb. 22, 1892 — Christ identified as "the great I AM"
- ST, Jun. 27, 1892 — With the Father from the everlasting ages
- RH, Jun. 28, 1892 — "Co-equal with God"
- ST, Nov. 27, 1893 — He and the Father were of one substance
- Lt 92, Feb. 17, 1895 — God is an ever-present "I am"
- Lt 119, Feb. 18, 1895 — I AM means an eternal presence
- Lt 119, Feb. 18, 1895 — Christ was using great name of God– the I AM
- RH, Dec. 17, 1895 — One of infinite dignity
- MS 2, Feb. 9, 1896 — Life original, unborrowed

- RH, May 19, 1896 — All that is attributed to the Father…is attributed to Christ
- ST, Apr. 8, 1897 — Life original, unborrowed, underived
- MS 101, 1897 — Infinite and omnipotent
- MS 101, 1897 — The eternal, self-existent Son
- YI, Dec. 16, 1897 — From eternity complete unity with the Father
- YI, Dec. 16, 1897 — They were two, yet little short of being identical
- YI, Dec. 16, 1897 — Two in individuality
- DA, 24 1898 — It was Christ who spoke to Moses at burning bush
- DA, 469 1898 — The idea of the eternal presence had been claimed as his own
- DA, 470 1898 — Announced Himself as the self-existent One
- ST, May 3, 1899 — The existence of Christ is not measured by figures
- ST, May 3, 1899 — Jehovah is the name given to Christ
- Lt 79, May 10, 1900 — Infinite nature
- YI, Jun. 21, 1900 — The eternal self-existing Son
- MS 81, 1900 — The self-existent, eternal, unchangeable One
- ST, Aug. 29, 1900 — There never was a time when He was
- not in fellowship
- MS 132, 1902 — God always has been. He is the great I AM
- RH, May 6, 1902 — The Lord of Heaven
- MS 111, Oct. 22, 1903 — Not one in person
- RH, Apr. 5, 1906 — God essentially, and in the highest sense.
- RH, Apr. 5, 1906 — From everlasting to everlasting thou art God
- RH, Apr. 5, 1906 — Existed from eternity, a distinct person

THE HOLY SPIRIT

The Holy Spirit as a Person

"The Holy Spirit is the Comforter, in Christ's name. He *personifies Christ, yet is a distinct personality*."[73]

"The Comforter is called 'the Spirit of truth.' His work is to define and maintain the truth. He first dwells in the heart as the Spirit of truth, and thus He becomes the Comforter. There is comfort and peace in the truth, but no real peace or comfort can be found in falsehood. It is through false theories and traditions that Satan gains his power over the mind. By directing men to false standards, he misshapes the character. Through the Scriptures the Holy Spirit speaks to the mind, and impresses truth upon the heart. Thus He exposes error, and expels it from the soul. It is by the Spirit of truth, working through the word of God, that Christ subdues His chosen people to Himself.

"…Sin could be resisted and overcome only through the mighty agency of the Third Person of the Godhead, who would come with no modified energy, but in the fullness of divine power."[74]

"When God's people search the Scriptures with a desire to know what is truth, Jesus is present *in the person of His representative*,

---

[73] Ellen White, Manuscript 93, 1893; in *Manuscript Releases*, vol. 20, p. 324.
[74] Ellen White, *Desire of Ages* (1898), p. 671.

the Holy Spirit, reviving the hearts of the humble and contrite ones."[75]

"We have been brought together as a school, and we need to realize that the Holy Spirit, who is *as much a person as God* is a person, is walking through these grounds, unseen by human eyes; that the Lord God is our keeper and helper. He hears every word we utter and knows every thought of the mind."[76]

"If man, in acquiring the Christian graces, works on the plan of addition, God has pledged Himself to work in his behalf upon the plan of multiplication.... The work is laid out before every soul that has acknowledged his faith in Jesus Christ by baptism, and has become a receiver of the pledge from *the three persons*, the Father, the Son, and the Holy Spirit."[77]

"When you gave yourself to Christ, you made a pledge in the presence of the Father, the Son, and the Holy Spirit,—*the three great personal dignitaries* of heaven. 'Hold fast' to this pledge."[78]

"The Holy Spirit is *a person*, for he beareth witness with our spirits that we are the children of God. When this witness is borne, it carries with it its own evidence. At such times we believe and are sure that we are the children of God."[79]

---

[75] Ellen White, Manuscript 158, 1898; in *Manuscript Releases,* vol. 12, p. 145.

[76] Ellen White, Manuscript 66, 1899, p. 4; in *Manuscript Releases*, vol. 7, p. 299.

[77] Ellen White, Manuscript 57, August 12, 1900, p. 4; in *SDA Bible Commentary,* vol. 6 (Washington, D.C.: Review & Herald, 1956), p. 1074.

[78] Ellen White, Manuscript 92, September 22, 1901, p. 2; in *SDA Bible Commentary,* vol. 7 (1957), p. 959.

[79] Ellen White, Manuscript 20, 1906, p. 9; in *Manuscript Releases*, vol. 20, p. 68.

"The Holy Spirit has a *personality*, else he could not bear witness to our spirits and with our spirits that we are the children of God. He must also be a divine person, else he could not search out the secrets which lie hidden in the mind of God."[80]

Holy Spirit as Christ's Representative

"Although our Lord ascended from earth to heaven, the Holy Spirit was *appointed as His representative* among men…. Cumbered with humanity, Christ could not be in every place personally; therefore it was altogether for their advantage that He should leave them, go to His Father, and send the Holy Spirit to be His successor on earth."[81]

"If we will open the door to Jesus, he will come in and abide with us; our strength will always be reinforced by *his actual representative*, the Holy Spirit."[82]

"When Christ ascended to heaven, the Holy Spirit *took His place*, and was *a perfect representation of Him*. It is the work of the Spirit to minister the richest grace, and make it effectual in the hearts of God's people, that the elect may be gathered into one family."[83]

---

[80] *Ibid.,* p. 69.

[81] Ellen White to J. E. and Emma White, Letter 119, February 18 and 19, 1895; in *Manuscript Releases,* vol. 14, p. 23.

[82] Ellen White, "Extracts from Communications Dated July 30, 1894 and February 6, 1894," *General Conference Bulletin,* February 15, 1895, par. 6.

[83] Ellen White to J.H. Kellogg, Letter 126, December 18, 1898; in *Manuscript Releases,* vol. 21, p. 55.

The Presence of the Holy Spirit

"Let me tell you what I know of this Heavenly Guest. The Holy Spirit was brooding over the youth during the school hours; but some hearts were so cold and dark that they had no desire for *the Spirit's presence*, and the light of God was withdrawn. That heavenly Visitant would have opened the understanding, would have given wisdom and knowledge in all lines of study that would be employed to the glory of God. The Lord's Messenger came to convince of sin, and to soften the heart hardened by long estrangement from God. He came to reveal the great love wherewith God has loved the youth."[84]

"If you have solemnly covenanted with God, *in the presence of Christ and the Holy Spirit*, to act as a member of the royal family, a child of the heavenly King, you will not in your life lie against the truth you profess to believe."[85]

"The *presence* of the Father, the Son, and the Holy Spirit, the three highest powers in the universe and those in whose name the believer is baptized, is pledged to be with every striving soul."[86]

The Father, Son, and Holy Spirit

"I saw that they were in danger in the apostles' days of being imposed upon and deceived by false teachers; and men were chosen by the brethren, or church, who had given good evidence that they were capable of ruling well their own house, and

---

[84] Ellen White, Manuscript 16, 1896; in *Manuscript Releases*, vol. 19, p. 114.

[85] Ellen White, Manuscript 130, 1902; in *Manuscript Releases*, vol. 18, p. 104.

[86] Ellen White, "Morning Reflections," *Pacific Union Recorder*, July 2, 1908, par. 4.

preserving order in their own families; men that could enlighten those who were in darkness. Inquiry was made of God concerning them, and then, according to the mind of the church, and the Holy Ghost, they were set apart by the laying on of hands. Having received their commission from God, and having the approbation of the church, they go forth baptizing in the name of *the Father, Son* and *Holy Ghost*, and to administer the ordinances of the Lord's house, often waiting upon the saints by presenting them the emblems of the broken body and spilt blood of the crucified Saviour, to keep fresh in the memory of God's beloved children, his sufferings and death."[87]

[Ellen White made it clear in 1881, "praise" all three members of the Godhead, including the Holy Spirit.]

"Let cheerful freewill-offerings be brought to the Lord, let us consecrate to Him all that we are, and all that we have, and then may we all unite to swell the songs,—

> "Praise God, from whom all blessings flow
> Praise him, all creatures here below;
> Praise him above, ye heavenly host;
> *Praise Father, Son, and Holy Ghost.*"[88]

" 'If a man love me, he will keep my words; and my Father will love him, and we will come unto him,' ["We," that is, *the Father, Son*, and *the Holy Ghost*], and make our abode in him."[89]

---

[87] Ellen White, *Supplement to the Christian Experience and Views of Ellen G. White*, (1854), p. 18-19.

[88] Ellen White, "The New Year," *Review & Herald*, January 4, 1881, par. 18.

[89] Ellen White to A.T. Jones, Letter 44, April 9, 1893; in *Manuscript Releases*, vol. 9, p. 12.

"Before he left them, Christ gave his followers a positive promise that after his ascension he would send them the Holy Spirit. 'Go ye therefore,' he said, 'and teach all nations, baptizing them in the name of *the Father* [a personal God,] and of *the Son* [a personal Prince and Saviour], and of *the Holy Ghost* [sent from heaven to represent Christ]: teaching them to observe all things whatsoever I have commanded you: and, lo, I am with you alway, even unto the end of the world.' "[90]

"What a salvation is revealed in the covenant by which God promised to be our Father, His only-begotten Son our Redeemer, and the *Holy Spirit* our Comforter, Counselor, and Sanctifier! Upon no lower ground than this is it safe for us to place our feet."[91]

"The Godhead was stirred with pity for the race, and *the Father, the Son,* and *the Holy Spirit* gave Themselves to the working out of the plan of redemption. In order to fully carry out this plan, it was decided that Christ, the only-begotten Son of God, should give Himself an offering for sin."[92]

"*The Father, the Son,* and *the Holy Ghost,* powers infinite and omniscient, receive those who truly enter into covenant relation with God. They are present at every baptism, to receive the candidates who have renounced the world, and have received Christ into the soul-temple."[93]

---

[90] Ellen White, "Words of Comfort," *The Home Missionary,* July 1, 1897, par. 16.

[91] Ellen White, Manuscript 15, 1898; in *Heavenly Places,* p. 137.

[92] Ellen White, "An Important Letter," *Australasian Union Conference Record,* April 1, 1901; in *Counsels on Health,* p. 222.

[93] Ellen White, Manuscript 27a, April 19, 1900, p. 3; in *SDA Bible Commentary,* vol. 6 (1956), p. 1075.

" 'All power (in the sense of authority), is given unto Me, as Mediator between God and man,' Christ said. 'Go, teach, bring into discipleship, all nations. Give them the knowledge of the truth of My gospel, which is founded on truth. Lead them to understand that *the Father, the Son,* and *the Holy Ghost* are heaven's loving, powerful agencies for the accomplishment of the work of representing God in the world. Lo, I am with you in this work…' "[94]

"*The Father, the Son,* and *the Holy Spirit* are seeking and longing for channels through which to communicate the divine principles of truth to the world."[95]

"The heavenly host are filled with an intense desire to work through human agencies to restore in man the image of God. They are ready and waiting to do this work. The combined power of *the Father, the Son,* and *the Holy Ghost* is pledged to uplift man from his fallen state. Every attribute, every power, of divinity has been placed at the command of those who unite with the Saviour in winning men to God."[96]

"*Three distinct agencies*, the Father, the Son, and the Holy Ghost, work together for human beings. They are united in the work of making the church on earth like the church in heaven. They place the resources of heaven at the disposal of those who

---

[94] Ellen White to G. A. Irwin, Letter 93, July 3, 1900; in *Manuscript Releases*, vol. 16, p. 15.

[95] Ellen White to Dr. and Mrs. J. H. Kellogg, Letter 43, June 13, 1901; in *Manuscript Releases*, vol. 20, p. 308.

[96] Ellen White to the Brethren and Sisters of the Iowa Conference, Letter 134, August 27, 1902; in *Manuscript Releases*, vol. 7, p. 233.

will appreciate and impart these spiritual treasures, multiplying them by using them to the glory of God. The powers of heaven work with human beings on the plan of multiplication."[97]

"After the believing soul has received the ordinance of baptism, he is to bear in mind that he is dedicated to God, to Christ, and to the Holy Spirit. *These three* all cooperate in the great work of the covenant made by baptism in the sight of the heavenly universe. The Father, the Son, and the Holy Spirit receive the believing soul into covenant relation with God."[98]

"The waters cover the candidate, and in the presence of the whole heavenly universe the mutual pledge is made. In the name of the Father, the Son, and the Holy Spirit, man is laid in his watery grave, buried with Christ in baptism, and raised from the water to live the new life of loyalty to God. *The three great powers in heaven* are witnesses; they are invisible but present…. The work is laid out before every soul that has acknowledged his faith in Jesus Christ by baptism, and has become a receiver of the pledge from *the three persons* —the Father, the Son, and the Holy Spirit."[99]

"Our sanctification is the work of the Father, the Son, and the Holy Spirit. It is the fulfillment of the covenant that God has made with those who bind themselves up with Him, to stand with Him, with His Son, and with His Spirit in holy fellowship. Have you

---

[97] Ellen White, "God's Purpose for His People," Manuscript 27a, April 19, 1900, p. 22, unpublished.

[98] Ellen White, Manuscript 56, August 12, 1900; in *Manuscript Releases*, vol. 6, p. 163.

[99] Ellen White, Manuscript 57, August 12, 1900; in *SDA Bible Commentary*, vol. 6 (1956), p. 1074).

been born again? Have you become a new being in Christ Jesus? Then cooperate with *the three great powers of heaven* who are working in your behalf. Doing this you will reveal to the world the principles of righteousness."[100]

"After we have formed a union with *the great threefold power*, we shall regard our duty toward the members of God's family with a much more sacred awe than we have ever done before."[101]

"We are baptized in the name of the Father, Son, and the Holy Ghost, and *these three great, infinite powers* are unitedly pledged to work in our behalf if we will co-operate with them."[102]

"The Father, the Son, and the Holy Spirit, *the three holy dignitaries of heaven*, have declared that they will strengthen men to overcome the powers of darkness. All the facilities of heaven are pledged to those who by their baptismal vows have entered into a covenant with God."[103]

"The *three great and glorious heavenly characters* are present on the occasion of baptism. All the human capabilities are to be henceforth consecrated powers to do service for God in representing the Father, the Son, and the Holy Ghost upon whom

[100] Ellen White, "Christ's Prayer for us," *Signs of the Times*, June 19, 1901, par. 4.

[101] Ellen White, Manuscript 11, February 5, 1901, p. 4; in *SDA Bible Commentary*, vol. 6 (1956), p. 1102.

[102] Ellen White, "Our Supply in Christ," *General Conference Bulletin*, April 4, 1901, par. 16.

[103] Ellen White, Manuscript 92, September 22, 1901, p. 9; in *SDA Bible Commentary,* vol. 5 (Washington D.C.: Review & Herald, 1956), p. 1110.

they depend. All heaven is represented by *these three* in covenant relation with the new life."[104]

"The Comforter that Christ promised to send after He ascended to heaven, is the Spirit in *all the fullness of the Godhead*, making manifest the power of divine grace to all who receive and believe in Christ as a personal Saviour. There are three *living persons of the heavenly trio*, in the name of these *three great powers*—the Father, the Son, and the Holy Spirit—those who receive Christ by living faith are baptized, and these powers will co-operate with the obedient subjects of heaven in their efforts to live the new life in Christ."[105]

"… the Holy Spirit, who is *as much a person* as God is a person…"[106]

"In the name of whom were you baptized? You went down into the water in the name of the *three great Worthies in heaven*—the Father, the Son, and the Holy Ghost. In the name of the Father, and of the Son, and of the Holy Ghost you were buried with Christ in baptism; and you were raised up out of the water to live in newness of life…. Those who have been baptized can claim the help of the *three great Worthies* of the divine similitude."[107]

---

[104] Ellen White, Manuscript 45, May 14, 1904, p. 10; in *Manuscript Releases*, vol. 6, p. 389.

[105] Ellen White, "Testimonies for the Church Containing Messages of Warning and Instruction to Seventh-day Adventists," Manuscript 21, January 9, 1906; in *Special Testimonies,* Series B, p. 63.

[106] Ellen White, Manuscript 66, 1899; in *Manuscript Releases*, vol. 7, p. 299.

[107] Ellen White "Lessons from the Fifteenth of Romans," Sermon preached in Oakland, CA, October 20, 1906; in *Sermons and Talks*, vol. 1, p. 363.

"Here is where the work of the Holy Ghost comes in, after your baptism. You are baptized in the name of the Father, of the Son, and of the Holy Ghost. You are raised up out of the water to live henceforth in newness of life,—to live a new life. You are born unto God, and you stand under the sanction and the power of *the three holiest beings in heaven*, who are able to keep you from falling. You are to reveal that you are dead to sin; your life is hid with Christ in God. Hidden "with Christ in God,"—wonderful transformation. This is a most precious promise. When I feel oppressed, and hardly know how to relate myself toward the work that God has given me to do, I just call upon *the three great Worthies*, and say: You know I cannot do this work in my own strength. You must work in me, and by me and through me, sanctifying my tongue, sanctifying my spirit, sanctifying my words, and bringing me into a position where my spirit shall be susceptible to the movings of the Holy Spirit of God upon my mind and character. And this is the *prayer* that every one of us may offer."[108]

"The Holy Spirit indites all genuine prayer. I have learned to know that in all my intercessions, the Spirit intercedes for me and for all saints whose intercessions are according to the will of God, never contrary to his will. 'The Spirit also helpeth our infirmities;' and the Spirit, *being God*, knoweth the mind of God; therefore in every prayer of ours for the sick, or for other needs, the will of God is to be regarded. 'For what man knoweth the things of a man, save the spirit of man which is in him? even so the things of God knoweth no man, but the Spirit of God.'"[109]

---

[108] Ellen White "Lessons from the Fifteenth of Romans," Sermon preached in Oakland, CA, October 20, 1906; in *Sermons and Talks*, vol. 1, p. 367.

[109] Ellen White, "Faith Brings Light," *Signs of the Times,* October 3, 1892, par. 3.

"But they were not left to fight the battles in their own human strength. The angelic host coming as ministers of God would be in that battle, and also there would be the *eternal heavenly dignitaries—God, and Christ, and the Holy Spirit*—arming them with more than mortal energy, and would advance with them to the work, and convince the world of sin."[110]

"*The Father, the Son,* and *the Holy Ghost,* powers *infinite and omniscient,* receive those who truly enter into covenant relation with God. They are present at every baptism, to receive the candidates who have renounced the world, and have received Christ into the soul-temple."[111]

"*The Father, the Son,* and *the Holy Ghost,* the *eternal Godhead* is involved in the action required to make assurance to the human agent to unite all heaven to contribute to the exercise of human faculties to reach and embrace the fullness of the threefold powers to unite in the great work appointed…"[112]

"The obedient children of God *recognize* the law as a divine law, the sacrifice on Calvary as a divine sacrifice, and the Holy Spirit as their *divine sanctifier*."[113]

---

[110] Ellen White, Manuscript 130, November 27, 1901; in *Manuscript Releases,* vol. 16, p. 204.

[111] Ellen White, Manuscript 27a, April 19, 1900, p. 3; in *Manuscript Releases*, vol. 6, p. 1075.

[112] Ellen White, "A Change Necessary," Manuscript 45, May 14, 1904, p. 9-10.

[113] Ellen White, "What Shall I do to Inherit Eternal Life?" *Signs of the Times,* July 14, 1890, par. 3.

"Evil had been accumulating for centuries, and could only be restrained and resisted by the mighty power of the Holy Spirit, the third person of the Godhead, who would come with no modified energy, but in *the fullness of divine power.* Another spirit must be met; for the essence of evil was working in all ways, and the submission of man to this satanic captivity was amazing."[114]

"The prince of the power of evil can only be held in check by the power of God in the *third person of the Godhead,* the Holy Spirit."[115]

"Sin could be resisted and overcome only through the mighty agency of the *Third Person of the Godhead,* who would come with no modified energy, but in the fullness of divine power."[116]

"Christ determined that when He ascended from this earth He would bestow a gift on those who had believed on Him and those who should believe on Him. What gift could He bestow rich enough to signalize and grace His ascension to the mediatorial throne? It must be worthy of His greatness and His royalty. He determined to give His representative, *the third person of the Godhead.*"[117]

"The Spirit was given as a regenerating agency, and without this the sacrifice of Christ would have been of no avail. The power of

[114] Ellen White to "My Brethren in America," Letter 8, February 6, 1896; in *Manuscript Releases,* vol. 10, p. 63.
[115] Ellen White, "Special Testimonies for Ministers and Workers—No. 10, (1897); in *Special Testimonies,* Series A, p. 37.
[116] Ellen White, *Desire of Ages* (1898), p. 671.
[117] Ellen White, "The Outpouring of the Spirit," *Signs of the Times,* December 1, 1898, par. 2.

evil had been strengthening for centuries, and the submission of man to this satanic captivity was amazing. Sin could be resisted and overcome only through the mighty agency of the *third person of the Godhead*, who would come with no modified energy, but in the fullness of divine power. It is the Spirit that makes effectual what has been wrought out by the world's Redeemer. It is by the Spirit that the heart is made pure. Through the Spirit the believer becomes a partaker of the divine nature."[118]

"It is not essential for us to be able to define just what the Holy Spirit is. Christ tells us that the Spirit is the Comforter, 'the Spirit of truth, which proceedeth from the Father.' It is plainly declared regarding the Holy Spirit that, in His work of guiding men into all truth, 'He shall not speak of Himself.' John 15:26; 16:13.

"The nature of the Holy Spirit is a mystery. Men cannot explain it, because the Lord has not revealed it to them. Men having fanciful views may bring together passages of Scripture and put a human construction on them, but the acceptance of these views will not strengthen the church. Regarding such mysteries, which are too deep for human understanding, silence is golden."[119]

---

[118] Ellen White, "The Promise of the Spirit," *Review & Herald*, May 19, 1904, par. 3.
[119] Ellen White, *Acts of the Apostles*, (1911), p. 51-52.

Chronological Summary

Below is a list of statements made by Ellen White about the Holy Spirit, in chronological order.

- ExV, 19 1854 — Apostles baptizing in the name of the Father, Son and Holy Ghost
- 2T, 226 1869 — The divine Spirit
- 2T, 320 1869 — The divine influence of the Spirit of God
- 2SP, 136 1877 — Disciples baptized in name of the Father, Son, and Holy Spirit
- 3SP, 256 1878 — "An equivalent for his [Christ's] visible presence"
- RH, Aug. 28, 1879 — The divine witness of the Spirit
- RH, Jan. 4, 1881 — "Praise Father, Son and Holy Ghost"
- ST, April 3, 1884 — It is his office to present Christ
- ST, April 3, 1884 — Appoints his Spirit to be man's teacher and continual guide
- RH, Jan. 24, 1888 — The presence of the Comforter
- ST, July 14, 1890 — Their divine sanctifier
- RH, Jan. 27, 1891 — His office work
- Lt 11b, July 17, 1892 — The Spirit, being God
- Lt 16j, Sept. 2, 1892 — God, the eternal Spirit
- RH, Nov. 29, 1892 — The Holy Spirit is "as the personal presence of Christ"
- Lt 2d, Dec. 23, 1892 — "Comes personally by his Holy Spirit"
- BE, Jan. 15, 1893 — The Holy Spirit is Christ's "representative"
- RH, Jan. 17, 1893 — The Spirit is "the True Witness"
- Lt 44, April 9, 1893 — The Father, Son, and Holy Ghost make their abode in us
- MS 93, 1893 — The Holy Spirit "personifies Christ"

- MS 93, 1893 — The Holy Spirit "is a distinct personality"
- GCB, July 30, 1894 — Personating Jesus Christ
- MS 43, 1894 — Our Advocate that stands by our side
- HM, Dec. 1, 1894 — Supplies "the place of his presence"
- GCB, Feb. 15, 1895 — His actual representative
- Lt 119, Feb.18, 1895 — Appointed as His representative
- GCB, March 4, 1895 — The Holy Spirit is "the representative of God"
- Lt 77, 1895 — The Spirit is all divine in its agency
- Lt 8, Feb. 6, 1896 — The third person of the Godhead
- Lt 8, Feb. 6, 1896 — In the fullness of divine power
- MS 16, 1896 — This Heavenly Guest
- MS 16, 1896 — That heavenly Visitant
- MS 16, 1896 — The Lord's Messenger
- SpTE, 51, May 15, 1896 — The faithful and true witness
- Lt 126, 1898 — A perfect representation of Him [Christ]
- MS 158, 1898 — Jesus is present "in the person of His representative"
- MS 66, March 25, 1899 — The Holy Spirit is "as much a person as God is"
- CH, 222 1899 — Father, Son, and Holy Spirit gave Themselves [to the plan]
- Lt 78, Jan. 20, 1900 — The eternal agency of the Holy Spirit
- MS 50, March 28, 1900 — The Spirit pleads not for us as does Christ
- MS 27 1/2, April 19, 1900 — Father, Son, Holy Ghost present at every baptism
- MS 27 1/2, April 19, 1900 — Powers infinite and omniscient
- MS 27 1/2, April 19, 1900 — The threefold name
- MS 27 1/2, April 19, 1900 — Three distinct agencies
- MS 56, Aug. 12, 1900 — These three all cooperate

- MS 57, Aug. 12, 1900 — The three persons
- Lt 93, 1900 — Heaven's loving, powerful agencies
- COL, 419 1900 — The divine fullness
- MS 11, Feb. 5, 1901 — The great threefold power
- MS 11, Feb. 5, 1901 — The excellence of the Father, the Son and the Holy Spirit
- GCB, April 4, 1901 — These three great, infinite powers
- MS 92, Sept. 22, 1901 — The three great personal dignitaries
- MS 130, Nov. 27, 1901 — The eternal heavenly dignitaries
- Lt 134, Aug. 27, 1902 — Combined power of the Father, Son and Holy Ghost
- MS 130, 1902 — In the presence of Christ and the Holy Spirit
- MS 45, May 14, 1904 — The eternal Godhead – Father, Son, Holy Ghost
- MS 45, May 14, 1904 — Three great and glorious heavenly characters
- SpTB, 63 1905 — Spirit in all the fullness of the Godhead
- SpTB, 63 1905 — Three living persons of the heavenly trio
- MS 20, 1906 — The Holy Spirit a divine person
- Lt 296, Sept. 9, 1906 — Compensates for "the loss of His personal presence"
- 1SAT, 363 Oct. 20, 1906— The three great Worthies
- MS 95, Oct. 20, 1906 — the three holiest beings in heaven
- AA, 426 1911 — The divine Messenger

"Fearful perils are before those who bear responsibilities in the cause of God—perils the thought of which make me tremble. But the word comes, "*My hand is upon the wheel*, and I will not allow men to control My work for these last days. My hand is turning the wheel, and My providence will continue to work out the divine plans, irrespective of human inventions. Man's plans will be overthrown, and the Lord God of heaven will reveal His glory. *The Father, the Son,* and *the Holy Spirit* will work out Heaven's law. *These three great Powers have pledged themselves* to bring to nought the inventions of idolatrous human minds. They have put the *infinite treasures of heaven* at the command of God's struggling people."[120]

---

[120] Ellen White, *Manuscript Releases*, vol. 21 (1993), p. 391.

THE SPIRIT OF PROPHECY

In the context of this topic of Ellen White and the Godhead, some argue that Ellen White's writings have been adapted, edited, or added to by those who helped her in her work. To answer this allegation, we will quote from a personal experience shared by M.L. Andreasen in a chapel talk given in Loma Linda, California, November 30, 1948:

"A few weeks ago I spoke in Los Angeles at the White [sic] on the subject of the Spirit of prophecy. I have been asked to repeat that speech. I do not know that I can do that, but I'll do my best.

"I became an Adventist as a young man. I was not brought up an Adventist—you might say not a Christian either. When I accepted the truth, I accepted it without knowing all that was involved as a part of a general program.

"I soon came face to face with the question of the Spirit of Prophecy, as revealed in the writings of Sister White. I read her published volumes and found them to be very good, but I didn't find any special inspiration in them. Indeed, I did not know they were supposed to be inspired. However, I considered them very good writing. At that time I was taking work in Chicago University, and majored in English. As you can hear, I'm a foreigner. I came to America as a young man and hence did not grow up here. If I were American-born, I would be a teacher of English today, for I love the language.

"The first time I became conscious of the beauty of language and of poetry was when a teacher in the university quoted this line: 'How sweet the moonlight sleeps upon this bank.' I said to myself, 'The writer is evidently attempting to say that the moon is shining. Why not say so?' The teacher seemed to read my mind and almost quoted my thoughts when he said, 'You might ask why he didn't say that the moon is shining. That would be a fact, but it wouldn't be poetry.' Then he gave illustrations. The poet could have written, 'How sweet the moon shines.' That would have been better than the first statement. 'How sweet the moon shines upon this bank,' would be still a little better, but not yet poetry. But when he said, 'How sweet the moonlight sleeps upon this bank,' something happened to me. That moment I saw a beauty in poetry that I had not seen before, and as he enlarged upon it— that many things in this world could never be said except in poetry—then I woke up to the fact that I was losing out on something, and that men, real men, could love language and poetry without losing any of their manliness. This was a revelation to me and was the beginning of my love for language and poetry.

"In the hymn today we sang, 'The cedars of Lebanon bow at His feet; the air is perfumed with His breath.' That is poetry, a beautiful poetic representation. We are not to take such words in a literal sense, nor are we to make prose out of poetry in the Bible.

"I had read *Desire of Ages* before I came to the University of Chicago, where I took a class in the life of Christ. We had many books for collateral reading, and I chose *Desire of Ages* as one of them. This gave me an opportunity to read it carefully day by day. I found there a beauty of expression that caught my attention, and I said to myself, 'I do not see how Sister White could ever have written that; she was a woman of but little education, and hence would be unable to produce such a work.' I said to myself again and again, 'She never wrote that.'

"I was interested not only in her language, but also in her theology. If you have ever attempted to write on the life of Christ, you have no doubt found many places where it was easy to make a misstep. Chicago University was not at that time any more than now noted for its orthodoxy and correct theology, but some of the men had some good work on the life of Christ. As I read *Desire of Ages*, I found that Sister White had treated certain subjects in such a consistent way, avoiding some pitfalls and stepping over others, that I again said to myself, 'Sister White could never have written that.' In another class I was attending, I was asked to collect as many 'immortal lines' from Shakespeare as I could find. This gave me an idea. 'Why not try to find immortal lines in *Desire of Ages*?' I did this, and found more immortal lines in *Desire of Ages* than in Shakespeare. That may have been because of my limitation or prejudice. I shall leave that an open question.

"When I began to preach, I came directly face to face with the question of Sister White. If I were to teach others, I felt I must know for myself. Believing in direct action, I went out to California to see Sister White. She received me graciously and I stayed for some months. I told her what I had come for. She listened kindly to me and said that I might have access to her writings. I said, 'I am not interested in that which has been printed. I think I have read it all. I want to know in what form it was before it was sent to the printer." I believed at that time that her copyists and proofreaders had fixed it up, for it seemed certain to me that she could not have written it in the form it appeared in print. I had with me a number of quotations that I wanted to see if they were in the original in her own handwriting. I remember how astonished we were when *Desire of Ages* was first published, for it contained some things that we *considered unbelievable*, among others the *doctrine of the Trinity* which was not then *generally* accepted by the Adventists.

"Some of the quotations concerned theology, others I had selected for their beauty of expression. I wanted to see how these quotations looked before they were corrected by the proofreaders. So I was given access to the manuscripts. I stayed in California several months. Being a reasonably fast reader, *I read nearly all Sister White had written in her own handwriting.* I was particularly interested in the statement in *Desire of Ages* which at one time caused *great concern* to the denomination theologically: '*In Christ is life, original, unborrowed, underived.*' pg. 530. That statement may not seem very revolutionary to you, but to us it was. We could hardly believe it, but of course we could not preach contrary to it. I was sure Sister White had never written, 'In Christ is life, original, unborrowed, underived.' But now *I found it in her own handwriting just as it had been published*. It was so with other statements. As I checked up, I found that they were Sister White's own expressions.

"Were there no corrections made in her manuscripts? Yes, corrections were made. She wrote rather fast, yet her writing was quite legible. But she would make spelling mistakes at times. There were also errors in punctuation. To her, punctuation was a minor matter. At times she would leave out not only a comma and semicolon, but also periods. This would cause difficulty at times to decide where the period should be. In all cases where Sister White wrote by hand the manuscript would be taken by the copyist and commas or periods inserted; then it would be taken to Sister White for her approval or correction. In the final analysis it was her work all the way through.

"In the mornings I would often sit with Sister White and visit. She began her work early, as you will find mentioned in her writings again and again. She got up at six o'clock, or at five, or four, and even earlier.

"As I asked her all manner of questions she would sometimes say, 'My mind does not work along that line today.' At other times she was ready to speak on almost any subject. I was pleased to find that Sister White could both smile and laugh. I had thought of her being always serious. I confess that to begin with I was a little scared, but tried not to show it. I found her to be very congenial, with a delicate sense of humor. At times she would laugh, not one of those heavy laughs which we sometimes hear, but a tingling, girlish, beautiful laugh."[121]

---

[121] M. L. Andreasen, "Chapel Talk," Loma Linda, California, November 30, 1948, emphasis supplied; in Document File 961, James White Library, Andrews University, Berrien Springs, MI.

AMAZING FACTS
MINISTRIES

1-888-402-6070 Office

Amazingfactsministries.com

Thank you for your kind support of Amazing Facts Ministries Inc. Canada!
We at Amazing Facts Ministries believe that we are living in the final days of earth's history. The last message of mercy for mankind is being sounded throughout the earth. We pray for heaven's wisdom to know truth and to sound the closing message to every nation, kindred, tongue, and people.

*"We are living in a time when **the last message of mercy**, the last invitation, is sounding to the children of men. The command, "Go out into the highways and hedges," is reaching its final fulfillment. To every soul Christ's invitation will be given. The messengers are saying, "Come; for all things are now ready." Heavenly angels are still working in co-operation with human agencies. **The Holy Spirit** is presenting every inducement to constrain you to come. Christ is watching for some sign that will betoken the removing of the bolts and the opening of the door of your heart for His entrance. Angels are waiting to bear the tidings to heaven that another lost sinner has been found. The hosts of heaven are waiting, ready to strike their harps and to sing a song of rejoicing that another soul has accepted the invitation to the gospel feast."*
Christ's Object Lessons - E.G. White, p.237.2

We wish you Heaven's Eternal Peace.

All donors will receive a tax-deductible receipt.

Notes:

Notes:

Notes: